# Contents

Words printed in **bold** appear in the glossary.

# Mohandas and Kasturbai

Mohandas Karamchand Gandhi fingered the **garland** of flowers which hung around his neck. He glanced nervously at the pretty girl who sat beside him on the wedding platform.

The boy's hand trembled as he offered her the sweet wheat cake, a **symbol** of the happiness they would share. It was no wonder he was nervous – this was his wedding day.

# Life Stories
# Gandhi

**Peggy Burns**

*Illustrated by Adam Hook*

# Life Stories

Louis Braille
Christopher Columbus
Grace Darling
Guy Fawkes
Anne Frank
Gandhi
Helen Keller
Martin Luther King
Nelson Mandela
Florence Nightingale
Shakespeare
Mother Teresa

**Cover and frontispiece** *Mahatma Gandhi, the Great Soul.*

Editor: Anna Girling
Consultant: Nigel Smith
Designer: Loraine Hayes

This edition published in 1996 by
Wayland (Publishers) Ltd

First published in 1993 by
Wayland (Publishers) Ltd
61 Western Road, Hove
East Sussex BN3 1JD, England

**British Library Cataloguing in Publication Data**
Burns, Peggy
Gandhi.—(Life Stories Series)
I. Title   II. Series
954.03092

**HARDBACK** ISBN 0–7502–0724–8

**PAPERBACK** ISBN 0–7502–1933–5

Typeset by Dorchester Typesetting Group Ltd
Printed and bound in Italy by G. Canale & C.S.p.A., Turin

wondered if she was frightened, too.

The young couple's parents had been planning this wedding since both children were small. It was 1882 and they lived in India. At that time in India people often married very young.

*Mohandas (right), aged 17, with his brother. He was a nervous boy.*

*Mohandas with his young wife Kasturbai.*

He and Kasturbai, his little bride, were both just thirteen years old.

Out of the corner of his eye, he looked at her again. Her head was bent low, so he could not see her face. But he

Mohandas was a quiet, shy boy. He was afraid of ghosts and terrified of snakes. He would not go to bed without a light in the room.

How he wished he was brave and strong, like some of the boys he knew at school! But from now on, there would be Kasturbai. She would be his friend. There would be no need to be afraid any more.

**Above** *The house where Gandhi was born. This beautiful temple has been built over it.*

# Study hard!

'If you want to do well for yourself and your family', said a friend, 'you need to study hard and become very clever.'

The eighteen-year-old Gandhi sighed. He wanted to be a **lawyer**, and that would mean years of study. He had heard that England was the best place to study law. But how could he go to England? It would cost too much. Besides, he was told that going to England would be against his **religion**.

But Gandhi's family talked it over. They thought he should go. Although they were not rich, they scraped together the money.

*When he went to England, Gandhi wore western clothes.*

Kasturbai was very sad when her husband said goodbye to her and to their new baby son, Harilal. On 4 September 1888, he sailed from the port of Bombay.

The huge, crowded city of London was very strange to the young man. Gandhi was more used to bullock carts than the horse-drawn **trams** of London. The English way of life was very different from life in his Indian village. He was homesick. He felt like giving up his studies and going home, but he stuck it out.

He was glad when his three years of study were over. The day after he passed his exams and became a lawyer, he set sail for India.

*The hurry-scurry of London made Gandhi feel lost and lonely.*

# Hate kills – love heals

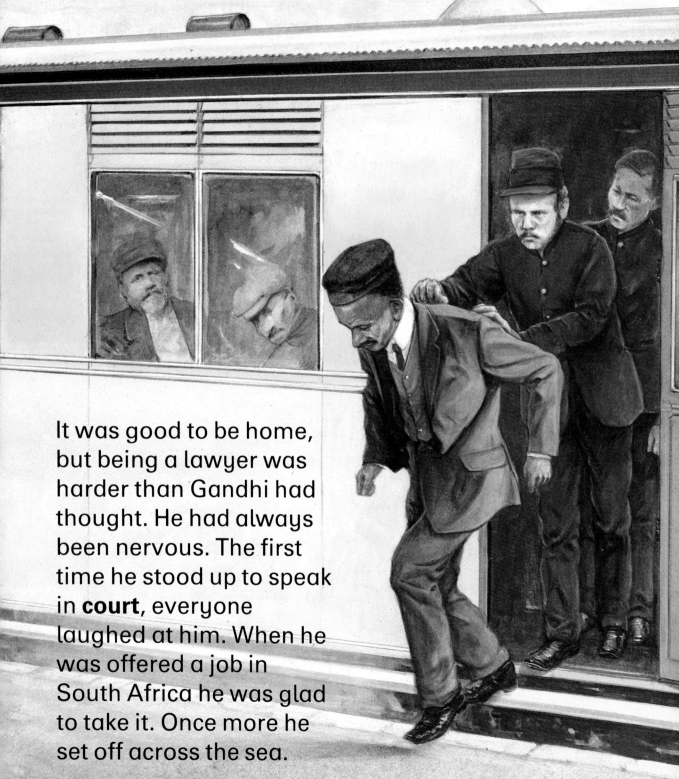

It was good to be home, but being a lawyer was harder than Gandhi had thought. He had always been nervous. The first time he stood up to speak in **court**, everyone laughed at him. When he was offered a job in South Africa he was glad to take it. Once more he set off across the sea.

Once there he worked hard. Before long, though, he realized that the many Indians living in South Africa (there were about 90,000) were treated almost like **slaves** by the **government**, which was made up only of white people.

***Gandhi outside his office in South Africa.***

One day, Gandhi himself was grabbed and thrown roughly off a train by police and railway guards, even though he had a ticket to travel **first class**. He found out later that all dark-skinned people were supposed to travel third class, which was very uncomfortable.

That night, as he sat shivering on the chilly railway platform, Gandhi decided to try and stop this unfair treatment. He also decided that this must be done in a peaceful way.

From then on, Gandhi tried to help other Indians who were being badly treated, and spoke out against unfair laws. He got over his nerves and became good at making speeches.

'It's better to die than to give in to bad laws,' he told a great crowd of people. 'We won't fight with guns and swords, and we won't hate the white government. But we will not do as they tell us any more.'

The struggle lasted many years. Gandhi and hundreds of Indians were arrested. Some even died in prison.

*Gandhi set up a printing press to print a newspaper, the* Indian Opinion, *for Indians in Africa.*

in the end Gandhi won. One by one the worst of the unfair laws changed.

When at last he returned to India, in 1915, he was welcomed as a great hero.

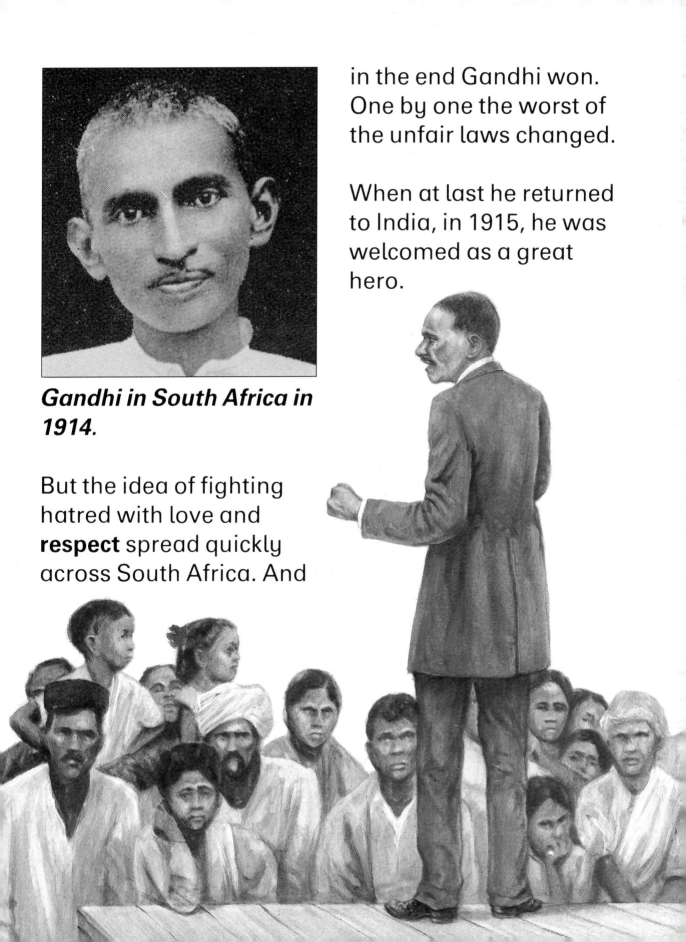

**Gandhi in South Africa in 1914.**

But the idea of fighting hatred with love and **respect** spread quickly across South Africa. And

# Children of God

Most Indian people belonged to one of two religions; they were either **Hindu** or **Muslim**.

Some people of the Hindu religion were called untouchables, and did all the dirty jobs.

*Untouchables – like this woman – were looked down on by other Hindus.*

Other Hindus found even their touch dirty.

Gandhi was himself a Hindu. But he refused to believe that one person was worse than another simply because he or she had been born an untouchable. He tried to teach people to love each other. He called the untouchables the *Harijans*, meaning Children of God.

*A few of Gandhi's simple possessions.*

14

*For most of his life Gandhi was a strict vegetarian.*

'Hindus, Muslims, **Christians** – all should love each other and respect what the other person believes,' Gandhi said.

Many Hindus do not eat meat because they think it is wrong to kill animals. Gandhi grew up as a **vegetarian**. He and his family lived simply and ate simple food such as fruit and vegetables. He often **fasted**, going without food for days at a time.

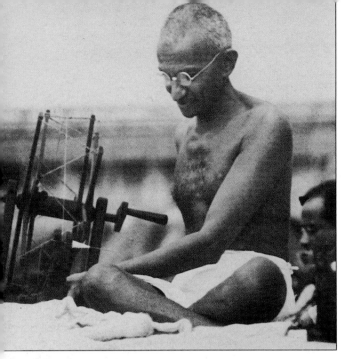

Gandhi even learnt to spin thread on a spinning-wheel because he thought that the people of India should make things for themselves rather than buy them.

**Gandhi tried to find time every day to spin a little cotton thread.**

But Gandhi could not settle down to live at home peacefully. He had work to do.

# 'We must be brave'

At that time Britain ruled India and made all the laws. The British had laid roads and railways across the country and built hospitals and schools, all of which was very good. But they also made the Indian people pay high **taxes**. Some British people treated the Indians very badly.

*The British in India laid railways and carried out other work.*

Many Indians thought that they should rule India themselves. They wanted to improve things in their own way, not Britain's.

Gandhi believed India could become free from Britain.

'We can force the government to set India free,' he said. 'Not by fighting with them, but simply by refusing to obey the laws they make.'

He travelled around, speaking at crowded meetings. He told people to take no notice of British laws and to stop paying taxes.

'They will attack us, and throw us into their prisons,' Gandhi said. 'They might even kill us!

But we must be very brave. We must never fight back, even if we have to die to set our country free!'

And many of them did die.

*A crowd of Indian women protesting against British rule.*

One day, in 1919, a great crowd of people met in the square in the town of Amritsar. British soldiers were ordered to march into the square. There they fired their guns into the crowd. Hundreds of people were killed.

*The police used frightening methods to break up crowds of protesters.*

# The salt march

The British had made a law which said Indian people were not allowed to make their own salt. Instead, they had to buy it from the government.

In a hot country like India, everyone needs salt. It keeps people healthy.

Gandhi knew of a place by the sea where salt lay on the sand. He decided that he would break this unfair law.

He and thousands of people marched to the sea. They went down to the water's edge where the salt lay.

*Many thousands of people marched to break the salt laws.*

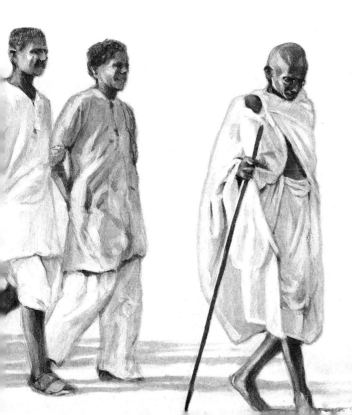

Gandhi stooped down and picked up a handful of salt. Cheering loudly, everybody else did the same.

The police arrested a lot of people, but nothing else happened.

21

Gandhi realized that more action was needed.

'We will march to the salt works,' he said, 'and take it over in the name of the Indian people.'

More than two thousand people marched to the salt works. Policemen, armed with long, metal-tipped poles, guarded the factory entrance.

The marchers came on. As they neared the gates, the police attacked, clubbing them to the ground with their poles and kicking them until the ground turned red with their blood. Not one of the marchers fought back.

Gandhi was sent to prison, but later the law about salt was changed.

*These women are making salt from sea water. This was against the law.*

# The Great Soul

In 1931, Gandhi was invited to London to talk to the British government about India's future. He went there with great hopes. As usual, he dressed in his simple **loincloth** and shawl.

*Gandhi in London.*

He even wore them when he went to meet King George V at Buckingham Palace. 'The King wore enough for both of us,' he joked afterwards.

But when he returned home, still no promises had been made about India.

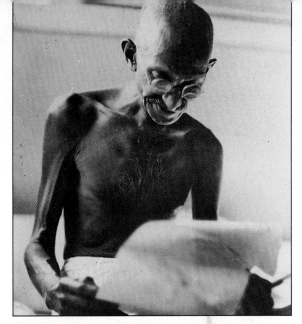

*Gandhi fasted often and grew very thin.*

Crowds of people turned out to welcome him home. Many Indians had begun to call him Mahatma, which means Great Soul.

But the British were afraid of him. For much of the time they kept him locked up in prison. Kasturbai, too, was arrested and was in prison with him when, after nearly sixty years of marriage, she died in his arms.

All through the **Second World War**, Gandhi carried on his fight for India. He went on many fasts, to show his dislike of British rule.

*Much damage was done in the fighting between Hindus and Muslims. These houses were ruined in riots.*

But as the struggle continued, Indians began to fight among themselves. Hindu and Muslim Indians attacked and often killed each other. Many people said India should be split in two. One part would be for Muslims and the other for Hindus.

But Gandhi was against this. He wanted all Indians to be friends. He told the people: 'We are all brothers.'

25

# 'I will not eat until there is peace!'

At last, in 1947, the British made India free. But it was not the great victory that Gandhi had wanted. The country was split into Hindu India and Muslim Pakistan.

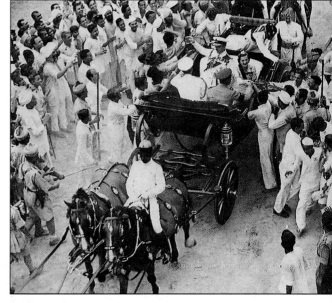

*India at last became free from British rule. There were great celebrations.*

Still, Hindus and Muslims attacked each other. Gandhi decided that there was only one thing he could do to stop them killing one another.

He would not eat until there was peace.

He began to fast, as he had done many times before. But this time, he was willing to die to bring an end to the fighting. He drank only water and he became very ill.

The two sides agreed to stop fighting just in time to save Gandhi's life.

*Before his fast, Gandhi ate a last meal of bread, fruit and goat's milk.*

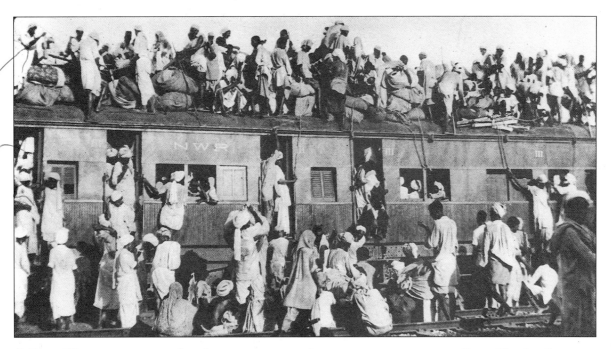

*Muslims crowded on to trains to escape the fighting.*

# 'Hai Ram!'

Not everybody agreed with Gandhi's teachings. Some Hindus began to hate him because he said they should live together in peace with Muslims.

*Gandhi's grand-daughters looked after him to the end of his life.*

It was 1948. Gandhi sensed that he did not have long to live. He spoke often to his friends about his own death.

It came during a prayer meeting. A man pushed roughly through the crowd and bowed in front of Gandhi. Then three shots rang out from the gun the man carried. Gandhi was hit by all three bullets.

'Hai Ram! – Oh Lord God!' he cried, as he fell to the ground. Mahatma Gandhi – the Great Soul – died with the name of God on his lips.

***This beautiful memorial was built on the spot where Gandhi's body was cremated (burned).***

But Gandhi's ideas live on. He believed all killing was wrong. And he showed that it was possible to bring change by peaceful actions. Other people around the world have followed his example.

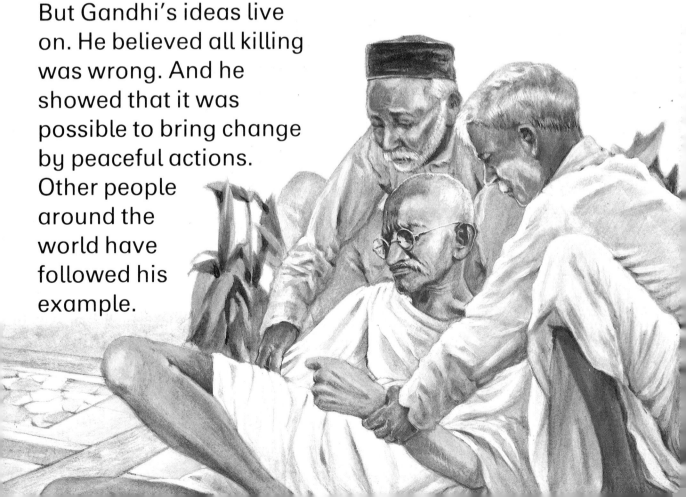

# Glossary

**Christians** Members of the Christian religion. Christians follow the teachings of Jesus Christ.

**Court** A room where people decide whether someone has broken the law.

**Fast** To go without food.

**First class** The most comfortable way to travel by public transport.

**Garland** Flowers hung round a person's neck.

**Government** The group of people who rule a country.

**Hindu** A member of the Hindu religion. Hindus believe that God has many forms.

**Lawyer** A person who has studied the law and makes a living from giving advice to others.

**Loincloth** A cloth worn around the hips and drawn between the legs.

**Muslim** A member of the Muslim religion. Muslims believe in one God, Allah.

**Religion** The worship of a god or gods.

**Respect** Politeness and kindness to other people.

**Second World War** The war that was fought in many countries between 1939 and 1945.

**Slaves** People who are owned by someone else and forced to work.

**Symbols** Objects that stand for something else.

**Taxes** Charges of money that people have to pay to a government.

**Tram** A kind of bus that runs on rails in the road.

**Vegetarian** A person who does not eat meat.

# Date chart

**1869** 2 October Mohandas Karamchand Gandhi is born.
**1882** Marries Kasturbai Makanji.
**1888** Sails to England to study law.
**1891** Becomes a lawyer and returns to India.
**1893** Takes a job as a lawyer in South Africa.
**1915** Settles again in India.
**1919** More than 400 people killed by the British at Amritsar.

**1930** Organizes salt march.
**1931** Goes to London for talks on India.
**1944** Kasturbai dies in prison.
**1947** India is freed from British rule but is split into two countries, India and Pakistan.
**1947** Gandhi goes on a fast because of fighting between Hindus and Muslims.
**1948** 30 January Gandhi is shot dead.

# Books to read

*Gandhi* by Nigel Hunter (Wayland, 1986)
*Gandhi* by Brenda Clarke (Cherrytree, 1988)
*The Ganges* by David Cumming (Wayland, 1993)

*Hindu Festivals* by Jane Cooper (Wayland, 1989)
*The Story of the Hindus* by Jacqueline Suthren Hirst (Cambridge University Press, 1989)

# Index

**Picture acknowledgements**
The publishers would like to thank the following for allowing their photographs to be reproduced in this book: Camera Press 5 bottom, 14 right, 19; Hulton-Deutsch 9, 11, 13, 15, 16, 23; Ann and Bury Peerless 6, 29; Popperfoto 7, 14 left, 18, 21, 22, 25, 28; Topham 5 top, 12 top, 17, 24, 27 top; Wayland Picture Library cover and frontispiece, 12 bottom, 26, 27 bottom.